Lyrical Tales: Collected Poems and Photography

Jennifer Word

EMP Publishing
www.emppublishing.com

EMP PUBLISHING
Salem, Oregon

Lyrical Tales: Collected Poems and Photography

ISBN: 978-0-6926382-4-8

EMP Publishing
Find us online at www.emppublishing.com

Cover design by Amygdala Design
www.amygdaladesign.net

ISBN: 0692638245 (paperback)
ISBN-13: 978-0-6926382-4-8 (paperback)

Printed in the United States of America

Dedicated to Barbara Bernard, Jack Klauschie, Dennis Goff, Kay Withers, Linda Terry, and Virginia Johnson. Six souls who, over the course of my life, inspired, encouraged, and pushed me to explore my artistic side, in any and all facets of the creative arts. Each of you in turn, and in your own fashion, taught me to be proud, unafraid, and unapologetic of the artistic fire within. A very heartfelt thank you goes out to each of you, and a humble and endless gratitude for being graced by your energies and auras, for however briefly. You each touched my days, made them better, and filled my life with light. You changed my life in positive ways, and I will forever be held in your debt. My life has been all the more rich by being blessed to have known each of you, and call you not only 'teacher', or 'director', or 'aunt', but also, 'friend'.

Contents

Introduction...i

Aurora's Gold...1

Grave (an Ode to Shakespeare).........................6

For Marc..8

White Corridors...11

Too Late...13

New Definition..15

Among Saints...16

Invocation...18

Free...20

A Poetica (Wish)..22

Landscape...25

Malady...26

Love Always...28

Mine..31

No Big Deal..33

Periphery...34

Not There..36

Our Time...37

Progress..38

Rape..39

Contents Continued

Starting to Realize.................................41

Respect...43

Secret Admirer......................................45

Ring the Bell..46

Subjugated...47

R.I.P...48

State of Being.......................................49

Best Thing…...50

The Day I Lost......................................52

Foreshadowing......................................53

Land of You..54

The Other Side......................................55

Too Long...56

Torn Between.......................................57

Try..58

Children's Halloween Moral.......................60

Always, Alexander................................63

I Wanna Talk Like Good Will Hunting............65

Sparkler...67

Entombed...68

About the Poet.......................................70

"I am…I was!"

–Gigolo Joe (*A.I. Artificial Intelligence*)

Introduction

This is my life's poetry. The earliest poem in this collection, *Children's Halloween Moral*, was written at age ten. The latest poem in this collection (not the last in order, but of age) would be *Sparkler*, written at age thirty-five. As of the publication of this book, I have not written any new poetry in over five years. Is it a coincidence, however, that at age forty, I am publishing every poem I ever wrote (that is even remotely worth publishing) and that the total equals exactly forty? Who knows?

On the subject of my photography, I do not claim to be a professional. It is an amateur hobby at best, a poor habit at the least. Further, I do not claim that any of the photographs appearing in this collection are of high caliber or quality. I will profess, however, to having a 'style'. While some of the photographs I have chosen to include in this small book were, indeed, what could be deemed happy accidents, others were wholly intentionally made to look out of focus, off-kilter, or simply overly pixelated. YES, you read that right. I intentionally took certain photos with sun flares knowingly blurring or otherwise distorting the main focus or subject of the scene, or otherwise purposely snapped my photos while in slight motion, to create a sense of vagueness, light streaks, or other similar 'mistakes' intended to invoke a general feeling of unease, frustration (and hopefully even at times a slightly subliminal) suggestion that something's just a bit "off" in this scene, or invokes an emotion of emptiness, hopelessness, disorientation, or conversely, a sense of hope, renewal, rebirth, strength, and even euphoria.

If you don't believe me on these 'intentional mistakes' I'll only briefly offer up the photograph used with the poem *Free* as an example. The poem itself is about (for me, anyhow) the feeling I believe every human being faces at least a few times over the course of their life, that they simply do not fit in. They don't belong. And for me, the phrases I find myself repeating mentally time and time again, "I don't even feel like I'm actually human. I feel like I'm an alien." Well then, what better photo than the one I selected from my purposely out of focus collection? That sign on U.S. Route 6 (coming in from the Warm Springs, NV side) is so interesting. The sign itself is a work of art, a testament to the human condition and our need to leave our mark on the world, in any way that we can. The sign is more covered in stickers left by visitors than there actually remains any visible sign. Save for the words "Extraterrestrial

Highway", the sign is virtually nested in a collage of human existences, screaming, "I was here!" At least, that's what **I** saw. I tend to see art in nearly everything I glance upon, but I digress. The sign is simply too interesting to snap in perfect focus. That would make something that is far from mundane a simply boring object. Sometimes clarity is too generic. As luck would have it, we arrived at the entrance to U.S. Route 6 (leading into Highway 375 and Rachel) in the early afternoon, and the sun was at a perfect angle behind and just to the upper left of the sign. I realized that if I slightly moved my body while snapping the photo in motion, not only would the sign be just slightly out of focus (but not gravely so, as you can still clearly read the words "Extraterrestrial Highway"), but it would also create a desired (for myself) effect of blurring the rays of sunlight, creating slightly rainbow-colored lens flares across the sign and the tree to the upper right. The desired result for me was a gratifying, if slight, exaggeration of a seemingly 'normal' scene, to invoke the feeling of 'alien-ness'. If this sounds complicated, you have no idea how many times I had to snap that photo while slightly in motion, to finally capture the one image with the proper 'mistakes' I was purposely trying to create, keeping certain things out of focus, while others still only just slightly off, for the sign still needed to be read and understood. Sigh.

So keep that in mind, with the viewing of each blurry, off-center or otherwise seemingly 'crappy' photo you view at the end of each poem in this book. What might, at first glance, indeed look amateur, isn't necessarily as cut and dried as what would seem to meet the eye. Not all the photos are shit. Not all of them are good. Most are just run-of-the-mill photos any yahoo can capture on their mid-range priced cell phone. But some of them actually had quite a bit of thought and work put into them, in the taking. And none of my photographs have been manipulated after the fact. That's just not my own personal style. I manipulate my photos *while* taking them, not after, because, to me, that's more fun, and for me, it's also more real and involved. *Interactive and physical.* There's what I see with my eye, and then there's the art it draws inside my mind. I try to take my photos to reflect an equal mix of both.

As for my poetry, I also do not profess to be an expert. I just write what I feel. And I am one of those "Hallmark"-type rhymers, folks. Yes, I prefer heavily metered stanzas, with every line, or every other line ending in rhyme. Again, it's just my own personal style. But I do not enjoy the backlash in modern times against poets who rhyme. Some of the greatest poets in history (or what many 'academics' themselves profess to believe are the greatest) wrote in rhymed verse. Shakespeare epitomizes the rhyming style. The Bard wrote nearly every play in metered stanzas with heavily structured monologues of rhyming verse.

I am in no way whatsoever attempting to compare myself to the master that was the poet and playwright, Shakespeare. I'm just saying. Don't knock it just 'cause it rocks it. All the greatest songs in history (for song lyrics are verses of poetry) mostly rhyme. I just happen to be an avid lover of music. I feel it soothes the soul. I cannot imagine going an entire day without actively listening to music of some kind or another, with or without lyrics. Perhaps my love and passion for the structure of music, including metered lyrics is the main inspiration for my own personal poetry writing style, who knows?

I love music, I love stories, and I love art, including photography. Photographs, to me, tell such suggestive stories, or at least, they imply *possibilities*. And most song lyrics tell stories of passion, struggle, betrayal, and yearning. My favorite songs and poems are the ones that tell a full story, as well as other forms of art, even the pieces that beg the question, "what is the story behind that look on her face? That smile on her lips?"

Hence the decision to name my collection *Lyrical Tales*. My poems tell stories. So do the photographs. No matter how vague the words or images may appear, an entire story lies behind each. And most importantly, much like the plethora of assorted stickers plastered to that "Extraterrestrial Highway" sign, these poems and images are meant to relay one very simple fact of my life and my art: *That I was here*.

I traveled, I loved, I adventured, I explored, I fucked up, I hurt others, and I was, in turn, hurt. But I was here. I existed. I saw parts of the world, and this is how those parts appeared to my mind's eye and my emotions. Within the pages of this book are some of the stories of some of the myriad of different lives I have lived. For I have lived many different lives. Here are some of my stories.

Jennifer Word
Salem, Oregon
February 5, 2015

Lyrical Tales

Aurora's Gold

I was just a young lad when I first heard his tale.
Granddaddy was born '78, of the eighteen hundreds.
Nineteen, I was, that summer home from Yale,
Summer of '54, of the nineteen hundreds.

He was seventy-six, but his memory was a lad.
He had a legend to relate to his blood.
"Ever heard of the Skookum?" — I never had.
"That's too bad, 'cause you should."

~

'Twas a Skookum Indian, first found that gold,
Up in Rabbit Creek, though claim was laid by Carmack.
Result was the same, whether truth been told,
And they came in droves to take a whack.

I was among them, a lad your age, foolish and full of grit.
Tilling land and washing dishes, 'til fate bade me heed it.
Dreams were coming true up there, so it seemed,
I left Ojai Valley when destiny called me to greet it.

Another world awaited me, there on the Yukon River.
Landed in Skagway, I herded the Chilkoot Pass.
Through white, to Lake Lindeman, all a-shiver,
I landed at those waters a few toes less.

'Twas end O' winter, but cold as Hell.
I took to dredging those channels.
I recall an occasional whoop or yell,
And men dancing 'round in their flannels.

I can feel the wet cold in my fingers to this day,
And the biting silt stuck 'neath my nails.
I can hear the wolves' howls at night as they bray,
And see Aurora dance in lights as she sails.

The trickling stream was music to my ears,
And a Skookum told me legends of his tribe.
Of how Aurora got her name, though it changed o'er the years,
His spoken word to me was his scribe.

His tooth-gapped grin opened wide,
"She shines in the Heaven's, your waiting bride,
And blesses those who see her true beauty inside.
She punishes men who survive on pride."

Everything was beauty to my Skookum guide.
Arrivers came by dozens, as the weeks and months passed by.
Shot, frozen, robbed, beaten, and yes, many died.
Those Argonaut miners still had to try, as did I.

By day, I sought gold, by night, Her radiant glow.
I watched Aurora dance in her iridescent gown:
A Queen in the Heavens, and me, far below;
A King, without my golden crown.

And to this day, Her memory is strong.
Light-dance colors, like the trickling stream in music.
The perfume of birch and pine played a song,
And Her nightly appearance was my salt lick.

"She was placed as sentry, over the seekers,"
My guide repeated many times the tale.
"Centuries before came, the stronger and the meeker,
She rode a frozen tidal-gale."

"Those who seek her will not fail.
She seeks out a want that is fair.
She gives to those that acknowledge her there,
And bestows the beholder with riches beyond compare."

And son, I'll tell you now, that in that moment,
All false notions fell away.
Surrounded by stars, my thoughts were cogent.
I could think of only one thing to say.

"That there light is the true beauty of this Earth,

And this land that surrounds me, the same.
This place has embedded its spirit in my heart,
The Klondike, my soul laid claim."

"If I should walk this terra firma 'nother eighty year,
If riches a plenty I do find,
Nothing will ever remain as clear,
As this experience here that I've mined."

"For no light could ever shine as bright as Aurora,
Nor mystical wonders behold.
None shall set my heart on fire,
As bright as Aurora's gold."

In the dim light of a starry night,
While Aurora danced silent above,
I saw Skookum's smile flash quick and white,
"Aurora got her name from your love."

Very next day, She heeded my words,
For spoken in truth they were,
Troy ounces; it equaled ten pounds and a third,
That nugget rewarded by Her.

I never forgot Her, nor left Her behind,
I carry Her in my heart to this day.
That land and that place, are fixed in my mind,
And Heaven shall hold me at bay.

That afterlife will be on that river,
Gazing up at those Heavenly lights,
The night before She became my giver,
When never richer were my sights.

~

He died that winter, after telling his tale.
And I remember his story, still.
I finally knew how he'd paid for Yale,
And I cried at the reading of his Will.

I took that trek, many years later on,
Though it took me 'til now, and I'm sixty.
I spread his ashes on the banks of the Yukon,
While the scent of the pines made me tipsy.

I do not understand my late grandfather's love,
Nor the true rendering of his heart and soul.
But tonight I will watch the night skies above,
And I'll hope for the sight of Aurora's gold.

*Aurora's Gold won second place in the poetry category of the 2011 Authors On Eighth writing competition. The poem was subsequently published in the Klondike Sun, August 24, 2011 (Vol. 23, No. 9).

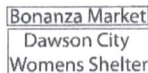

(Trees of Mystery – Klamath, CA)

Grave (an Ode to Shakespeare)

I was standing alone in my grave,
When the trees rustled their tune.
The birds sang in chorus,
A song of innocent June.
Little did they know,
That not long ago,
I was innocent too.
But society was jealous of me,
And one wicked admirer knew,
That not with him,
Yet with another,
An undying love bound me to you.
Tainted treats were obscurely placed,
Easily within my hand.
A sonnet from you,
Left me to coo,
But not for long to stand.
A twelve-man conspiracy,
Was deciding that your words to me,
Were all that was needed to judge.
The town was glad,
Our love made them sad,
So forever they held a grudge.
As the morning of judgment arrived,
The sun seemed so hard to strive,
To repair the storming day.
A shovel up against a tree,
Left me alone to see,
That life continued on its merry way.
As loose dirt crumbled down,
The sky seemed to frown,
At some unfortunate loss.
The clouds became angry,
The wind, obscene,
With no apparent cause.

~

Then he walked by,
With a saddened eye,
And found my lonely grave.
His knees fell down,
Upon the ground,
His heart too late to save.
With a dagger's eye,
He did not cry,
But softly spent his life.
'Tis sad, but true,
That parted, me and you,
Should come back together with a knife.
In he fell,
The clouds cried to tell,
The world of what he gave:
His life for me, for eternity,
Now together, forever,
In our grave.

Every grave tells a story. Morro Bay Cemetery. (Morro Bay, CA).

For Marc

It was your voice from across the distance,
That I hadn't heard in years…
And the words that issued from your mouth,
That nearly brought me to tears.

You told me all about your life,
And all that you'd been through,
Like reading a manual,
Some step-by-step "how-to."

And perhaps your life's progression,
Would seem a simple guess.
You play your role; do as you're told,
Saying 'no' would be in jest.

But if you could see yourself through me,
Perhaps you would change your mind.
And not say your life is nothing special,
With no surprises to find.

Yes, it is true; you take orders over there.
So I can live free, over here, without care.
You go where they send you,
And for that, I commend you.

Do you think that means
Nothing at all?
Not only in form,
But in your heart, stand tall.

If they sent you into war,
You would go without complaint.
And die for me, and for your country,
Straight into danger without restraint.

No, you are not unique,

From a certain point of view;
You are every mother's son,
mediocre as they come,
And following all the rules.

But I feel the need to tell you now,
How I see you – and others, too.
How a world of people you are not around,
Dream of heroes, and look to you.

Your name is not known, nor your face.
Your deeds go un-shown,
As the world keeps its pace,
And our country holds its place.

You are part of that,
Yes, more than some.
Willing to die for your cause,
Because that's how wars are won.

You are only a man, in a throng of thousands,
But don't ever say that you are nothing.
That your life is not special, or even unusual,
Because to me you are extraordinary.

If only you could see yourself through me.
And everything that shows.
You are my friend, I'll never forget,
And also one of my heroes.

Saint Mary's Veteran Cemetery (Ferndale, CA).

White Corridors

Will I hear the silence increase,
As your heart begins to fade?
Will I feel the unstoppable beat,
As nature undoes what it has made?

As I walk through white corridors,
And smell the cleanness of death,
I wonder what lies at the core,
After the very last breath?

I walk in a dream of darkness and light,
And wish to be awake.
I live in a world of wrong and right,
Where love is for life's sake.

For when the book is closed,
The words cannot be read.
And when we presuppose,
Then nothing can be said.

I know that time is silent,
And faster than my eye.
Why can't I stop it?
I just stand and watch you die.

Will I hear the end as it approaches?
Will I survive the pain as your life finishes?
Will I be intact when it is over?
As an era of wonder diminishes…

My Beloved Aunt and Grandmother: Two Lost Eras.

Too Late

It's never too late, so the saying goes,
But on those lips, Time will impose.
While others wane away from home;
Sleep weary, season dry as bone.

Others awake on an endless ride of analyzed regret,
Of a day (or week) without regard—trying to forget.
They ask themselves, still, could it be so?
Though opportunity passed a decade ago.

Lives are changed in a day, in a permanent way,
But it's never too late, they always say.
They have not walked *my* way.
Time is a game, of which not to play.

Nor underestimate its worth.
Mere minutes extinguish life or afford its birth.
And Hell's eternity, can an hour contain.
A lifetime, a day can hold.

A viewless thing is this power,
And illusionists are bold.
Yet all who survive to,
Will grow old.

It's never too late we all like to think,
Even while teetering on the very brink.
And happiness' cause is lost in a pause,
Wielded by the meek.

E=I-T² (EXIT EQUALS INDECISION MINUS TIME SQUARED)

New Definition

I pondered the reason why things were not right,
Why everything seemed out of place.
Three years passed by, I wondered why,
I could not find a trace.
Of familiar etchings, and similar sounds,
Of a time I knew before.
The minute fell down, the day struck out,
A stranger walked out the door.
Unfamiliar to myself am I, my own misgivings—lost.
As a world spins around (in my mind's eye)
Will I ever compile the cost?
This sudden knowledge. Something so strange.
Things never change, but merely—rearrange.

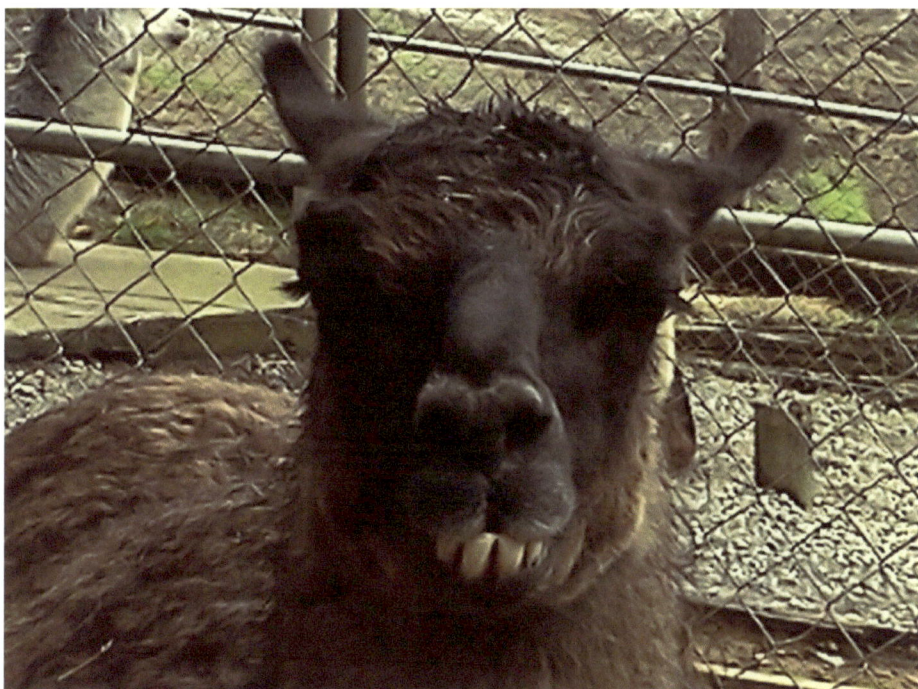

Redefine Beautiful—West Coast Game Park Safari (Bandon, Oregon)

Among Saints

Among saints in this place, I fall below grace.
Sinking into this pit, I love the feel of it.
Many fall behind comprehension, yet I seek imperfection.
To go where martyrs fall, to know the weight of it all.
Creating my choices, I hide from their voices.
To secure my vices, to *embrace* what entices.
I *must* go inside—I will *not* hide.
This crude mud; I digest—to feel the life inside this death.
The slick oil and disgust, after which I lust.
To create words from confusion, the depths of my own delusion.
Stripped, ripped and torn, is the true art of form.
The countdown, since my birth; understanding my own worth.
As I fall, I seek the destruction of this wall.
Well, shouldn't we all?

Unknown grave, Ferndale Cemetery (Ferndale, CA)

Drama & Darkness

Each day is the same. I wake up alone.
All I ever wanted was someone to hold.
Each time I try, fate finds a way,
To take all my chances, at love away.
With brief glimpses of warmth and sanctuary,
That forever I am burdened in my heart to carry.
The memories do not warm. Recollections do not brighten.
For me these hauntings only frighten.
Each day is the same. I wake up alone.
All I ever wanted was someone to hold.
Yet, each day I wake up to my life and its starkness.
Waiting for an end to this drama and darkness

Main Pier at Morro Bay (Morro Bay, CA)

Invocation

Be my Sun and Moon.
My Beloved Provocation.
Be my Night and Day.
Only grant my Invocation:

Take my Essence.
Become my God.
Bless me with Your Presence,
You Beguiling Charade.

Possess me,
Caress me,
Finesse me,
You taunting Fraud.

Bathe me in Dissension,
You're water turned to wine.
I hunger for your attention,
Creation of my Own Mind.

You Ghost, You Partition.
You conceived Apparition,
Phantom-Magician,
Specter-spirit of precision.

Adjoining, Approaching,
Nearing, Encroaching.
In my Creation. Imminently here.
Play inside the Cosmos of my Sphere.

Bring me to life. Be Bold.
Pour ignition on these flames.
Fire-fury, Grab hold,
In a Death-Dive—Untamed.

Make Your Mark, here where I stand.
And I will—in silence—cry.
Love, burn an Etching upon my hand.
And Thy will be done, I die.

Beauty & light, seen daily, too easily forgotten. Inside The Melting Pot restaurant (Thousand Oaks, CA)

Free

I was born with a perfect soul,
And a heart with a hole.
In a world full of wickedness
And a mind with a will of its own.

I've been bad, with the flick of a thought.
I've been grand, and I've prayed a lot.
With a body and mind going in two directions.
Imperfection is my genetic connection.

I don't want to be bad,
But I don't like being good.
With the way that I am,
I wouldn't think that I could.

I was hung on a cross with you.
You say I should be grateful with what I can do.
Born with flaws I should overcome,
But I'm rather tired of being like you.

You say I was born bad.
And I don't know what I have.
I have sinned, but I'm proud of who I am.
So I missed the mark, I did exactly what I can.

You say you'll take me to the Promised Land,
But I am who I am,
And I don't understand,
Why I strive for perfection, which I can't stand.

They say it's all worth it,
And I'll be thankful in the end.
Only the Lord Jesus,
Can be your true friend.

I don't know just what I need to be,
I'm bound for Heaven,
But sometimes…
I just want to be Free.

Ever felt like an alien? LIFE is not in focus. (Warm Springs, Nevada).

A Poetica (Wish)

So many things I write just to release my feelings.
The only thing that constantly rides me…
Thoughts of you.

It hurts to see how cruel you have become.
How all the things that once were important to you,
All the things you once loved,
Don't mean anything to you at all anymore.

Did you simply choose to forget?

You promised me this would not happen.
You said you would never hurt yourself.
You said you knew what was safe and what wasn't.
So why has your new 'mental state' left you…
Cold and indifferent?

How many people do you like now?
Do you even like yourself?
How easy is it now to concentrate…
Even for just a little while?

Go ahead and tell me now what you used to tell me.
Tell me it's not a habit.
Tell me you don't go out looking for it.
Tell me it's not out of hand.
Tell me you could stop if you wanted to…
But it's just too much fun.

I am not having any fun.
I was the one who believed your lies.
I was the one who ended up caring too much.
I was the one who got left behind…
To clean up your mess.

I see your old friends, who like I,

Miss you so much.
The you that doesn't exist anymore.
Where are you now?
Are you buried inside some deep crevice of your own mind?

Now you are blind.
Falling deeper and deeper into the hole you have dug.
All I can do is watch, since your mind no longer
Even recognizes me.

I feel so helpless.
This pain never goes away.
I deal with it every day.
It eats me up inside…
Like a horrid cancer uncontained.

It is you.
The new, cruel, horrible, cold and indifferent…
Altered you.

If only you could just step away and see.
But that is the trap.
You can never see.
Only the eyes of the outside victim see.

You were once someone who cared and loved.
You loved me once, until I got in the way.
Now your habit controls you.
It is a monster that you have invited in.
It will eventually destroy you.

You are poison in my soul…
You are poison now.

Until you kill the habit, everything you touch dies…

And I wish you had never touched me.

Love can make you feel so lost and alone—and unseen.

Landscape

The home I once loved, I now slightly hate.
As everything it made me I now debate.
And the beauty I saw, now seems a flaw,
Compared to the vast landscape of the world.
Every day is a fight to remain in a world of heartache and pain.
All the struggles seem in vain. Useless effort with nothing to gain.
As hopes and dreams go down the drain, I lose the final fight to remain
sane.

A foggy morning. (Salem, Oregon).

Malady

My affliction, my malady, non-existent to you.
Tendrils of cyclone memory, filling my heart with ache.
My audience—gone. My will—broken.
My world—unwatched by thee.
I am abandoned. I am without hope.
Did my eyes not shine bright enough?
Was my smile not infectious and affecting?
I am not worth one single care?
I thought I'd made a real friend.
My despondence warrants no concern.
When worlds collapse, and fears abound,
Where are you now?
Did you look upon me and see nothing?
I am not worth one small word.
If this hope is lost, my sanctuary is stolen.
What world is safe, with you not in it?
Not even a bother, not one small thought.
I was a storm inside your harbor.
You were a tempest inside my heart.
A gale to calm the incessant wind.
Caffeine high to complement the ingestion.
A listener, and a thousand questions.
A quiet mind, empty and satisfied.
Everything lost when I wasn't looking.
Catch me off guard with your forsaking.
Why have you left me all alone?
My presence, my proximity did not Create.
I am not worth your words of comfort.
I mean nothing to you at all.

Without Harbor. (Carmel by the Sea, California).

Love Always

Dispel the vagueness of meaning,
When we grow accustomed,
To arriving and leaving,
With the push of a button.

A keystroke, a signature,
And words that despair,
When we read, but don't see them,
For the feelings they bare.

A brief glance, a gloss-over,
Of something so precious,
Becomes a hardened cover,
To efforts so tedious.

An expression, perhaps to some,
But not to me.
These words contain the secret,
Of my heart's raging sea.

Does it mean to you,
What it means to me?

Is it a thoughtless expression,
From someone unobservant?
Of words and their weight,
And how we should serve them?

From this sky,
The wind blows me from you,
But not say goodbye,
Without proper adieu.

To choose something minute,
Not too overly bawdy,
That contains within it,

A power so Godly.

To express in two words,
What you mean to me, Dear.
To exclaim, and to fall,
Towards the extremity of fear.

That in my heart,
Forever you will be.
Though voices may halt,
From some misunderstanding.

Just leaf through our past,
And to the very last page,
And hold to it fast,
What those last words engage.

See that I think of you,
Though silence ensues.
And though insecurity brinks,
Let two words diffuse.

Know that I carry you with me,
Through all of my days.
From a message so simple,
With two words,

Love Always.

Countless Decades Old Tree Friends. (San Simeon, California).

Mine

Has it been so long…?
Have we forgotten our hearts?
With each year that brought us near,
Has the silence pulled us apart?

When we both are afraid of what we might say,
Or of how the other might take it.
Or say what we mean, leaving nothing unseen,
Yet, worry the other will mistake it.

The meaning of **I love you**.
The meaning of **my best friend**.
There's nothing you could ever do,
Or say to change that end.

So be extreme and even self-centered,
Go ahead and scream, act like a bastard.
Say something rude; tell me your views,
Ignore me for months on end if you choose.

Be selfish and tell me your needs.
Don't ever apologize for having your dreams.
All I see is you, beautiful and whole,
And I love your mind, heart, body and soul.

Forever in my heart, you will be.
I've told you countless times what you mean to me.
With every **I love you**. With every **letter**.
In all of my words, you should know better.

Speak your mind and let me in.
Your loftiest deeds, nor greatest sin,
Could ever make my heart un-won.
You are my friend for life; the deed is done.

There are no bounds, nor barriers,
Between the closest of friends.
Lest we create them, and perpetrate them,
And let the closeness end.

I take you as you are,
In every meaning of that line.
No matter how close, or far…
Whatever you give me, will be mine.

"To find beauty, kiss the flower. It will open." (Dream Voice).

No Big Deal

It's no big deal, I guess, but at the ripe old age of thirty-one,
I don't really like who I've become.

Emotionally almost dead, but I'm slowly coming back.
Came real close to dying, but I'm slowly coming back.

The dreams screamed at me. Think I've managed to revive them.
People will be disappointed in me. **I don't plan to be one of them.**

Don't know how, but someday I'm gonna have my dreams.
Don't know when, but someday I'll sew my soul back on at the seams.

A harbor full of kindred spirits. (Morro Bay, California).

Periphery

Enter, silent sorrow.
If not invited, plunge in.
Enter into the rose.
Evaporate the umbilical dew
Which prolongs her ethereal existence.
Acrimonious torrents of torsional pain
Strangle her life.
Relieve the unbearable panic
Of love and hate, at once.
Wretched rose!
Cast off your petals.
Black weeds haunt your memory.
Do not wear them to mourn.
Was your seed carelessly planted,
By hands that never plucked you?
Soil and sunlight do not carry
The nourishment of life
To your affection-starved core.
Chance to blossom,
Only to be invaded by a bee's caustic hunger.
Now the antagonist feeds no more.
And the rose has developed
A dependency for the evolutionary
Poison that taints her oppressed soul.
She cannot take flight.
The aesthetic rose remains motionless.
Violet patches of death
Elongate themselves inside veins of loneliness.
The garden is deceased.
The rose is deceived.
The bee is feeding somewhere.
Subtle breezes rattle
Shattered remains and shards of flora.
Sunlight frequents the Earth
With only host glances of tepid eminence.
The rose awaits her death.

As the last echoing calls of migrant
Hope desert the plane,
She does not cast off her petals.
The celestially sweet flower,
With all her excruciating days,
Folds her fan of memories
And regrets into a divine embrace.
Petrified now, for all the world to see.
Everlasting, Perennial Heart.
A legacy lies at her feet.
Periphery. Dormant seeds of time.
Silent sorrow blows on the breeze.
Abandoned life, renewed, restored.
Hopeful rays return once more.
Unchain the gates of ignorance.
Yet, enter again softly, silent sorrow,
For the bee, thirsty yet, awaits.

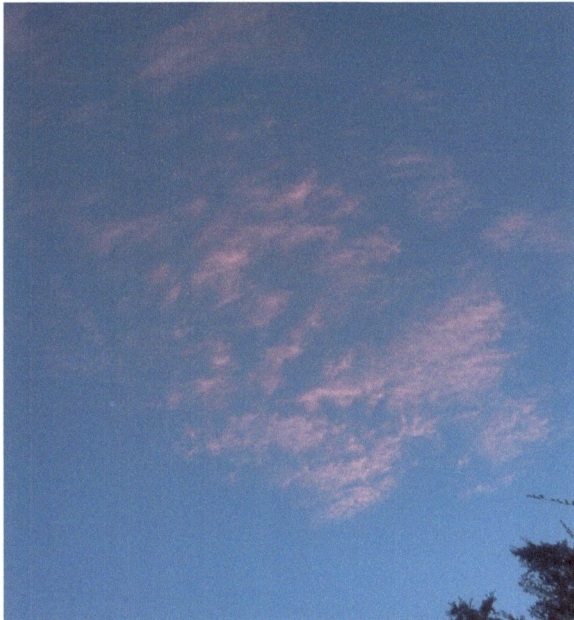

Periphery was my first poem back at it, at age sixteen, after *Children's Halloween Moral* at age ten. This was my last sunset in Oak Park, California, before moving away.

Not There

In Berkley, the whole world is yours.
Can you imagine a place, where they don't lock their doors?
Is it really a heaven? When three blocks away,
People are being violently slain.
Have you found your Utopia? When every day,
People's hearts are sacrificed away?
If I ask you what you think of it all, would you have anything to say?
The truth be told, you're much too old, and look the other way.
I'm glad I'm not like you, for all the pain it puts me through.
At least I know the world I'm in. You turn your back on everything else,
Do you turn your back on yourself?
You turn your back on me, and refuse to see the state of affairs.
You turn your back, and when you glance behind,
You see that I'm not there.

Sunset at deserted beach. San Simeon State Park. (San Simeon, California).

Our Time

If time could lapse and bring you to me.
If days were only minutes that ended so quickly.
Loneliness would have no hold over me.
If I could reach out across the distance, lightly touch your face.
Then space would mean nothing. It could not destroy my hope.
If I didn't feel your breath on my neck, or your presence guarding me,
The ocean would become a chasm. This land a bed of coals.
If you did not reach across all bounds, I would be lost.
Now that I have found you, and you know that I am here,
It is only the slow passing of time, that must end our space of waiting.
Someday, hand-in-hand: Together, will arrive. Our Time will be cast.
Inside a crushing embrace, we'll begin at last.

"R Time" boat, Astoria Harbor. (Astoria, Oregon).

Progress

Tell me what you believe; all the fears you have.
Is every single guilty feeling the cause of a man?
Where do you come from? Can you be so bold?
To decide whom you are, or let yourself be told.
Did you let him teach you right from wrong?
Did you let him create your mind?
Did you grow up singing *his* favorite song?
And always walk behind?
Who was the one that told you *no*?
Did they do it for your own good?
Now every time you hold back,
Do you do it because *he* said you should?
Delve into the darkest parts, to that secret, hidden place.
For every falter and hesitation, there *is* attached a face.
It began with your very first step, and then at your first kiss.
Every idea you thought was yours was really always *his*.
You think that it's over – you've managed to run and hide.
You never got away at all – just progressed from Daughter to Bride.

Simple circle decoration. Flavel House Museum. (Astoria Oregon).

Rape

You betrayed me,
Used me,
Abused me,
Invaded my mind.

You played me,
Invaded me,
Persuaded me,
Then left me behind.

You cast your hooks,
Baited me,
Hated me,
Evil of the worst kind.

You created chaos,
Had your fun,
When the apple was done,
Threw away the rind.

You committed a sin.
Fell from grace,
Then quickened your pace,
Left me an axe to grind.

You stole from me,
And I'm willing to bet,
You have not a single regret.
Forgiveness for you, I will never find.

Man-made water bowl for ground squirrels. Morro Bay Rock. (Morro
Bay,   CA).

Starting to Realize

She's reaching the edge, she's about to fall.
She's starting to drop things, giving up on it all.
This is not a simple death, nor a horrid tragedy.
It is the birth of an ugly thing. It is 'self-satisfying.'
It's because she's been pushed too far. She's starting to realize.
Seven years bad luck, a broken mirror; salvation's in her eyes.
It's no surprise. It's an age-old truth.
Too simple to see, and impossible to prove.
To those who've chosen ticky-tacky: Me like you, and you like me.
Because they refuse to see, they are their own worst enemy.
The world is dead, devoid of dreams. The weak now rule in packaged reams.
They surround the dreamers with hate, and stop us from living out our fate.
If you think it's your birthright, think again, and understand.
You'll have to scream and kick and fight, and get blood on your hands.
Nothing ever comes from being polite. You might have to break a heart or two.
You'll have to weigh the wrong and right, to get what really belongs to you.
Revelation is violent; it always was.
Revolution is silent; don't forget the cause.
She's thinking these things, but will she ever say them?
Will she be the one? To make herself a victim?
Or will she give in to this world, to "them" and all their people.
Remain un-free, sadly meek, and join the ticky-tacky feeble.

Make your mark, no matter how small or impermanent. Some *will* see. Dare to build differently. Ruby Beach. (Quinault, Washington).

Respect

Perhaps I was desperate? Alone and afraid.
No reason for suspicion of the friendship we'd made.
You moved in circles of the most elite.
You were my connection to join the fleet.
Beauty beyond compare, I watched men fall.
I wanted to *be you*; I wanted it all.
I listened to your stories with a sympathetic ear.
You turned on my worries and never shed a tear.
I copied your mannerisms, adopted your words.
I watched you destroy people in hordes.
When it came back to me, you were always so sweet.
I never complained, just lay down at your feet.
Ignoring the pain you brought in the end.
Until one day, you hurt a Friend.
When he cried, I heard his call.
There I heard the Truth of it all.
For two years I made you my example of lust.
Called you my friend; gave you my trust.
I was enveloped by *envy*. I hated myself.
Put my feelings up on a shelf.
Just to be near you, associated with *your* name.
Now to even know you brings me great shame.
To describe the anger I feel towards you:
It is almost impossible for me to do.
This is the worst feeling, to be let down.
This pedestal you stepped on, crumbling all around.
As I finally see what you really are.
So far from me, your beauty, marred.
I can never forgive you for this feeling I've kept.
I hate being disappointed. I hate losing respect.
If there is one thing I've found; one thing that I know:
As others remain, chained and bound, I now see myself as **whole**.

Old Church in the Ghost Town of Bodie. They say that if you don't leave an offering in the bowl inside the vestibule, you'll be cursed. (I left a quarter and an old keychain). They also say that if you take anything from the town, even a single nail, you'll also be cursed. I took nothing (except several photos). Two weeks later, my car broke down...**badly**. Coincidence? **Respect Bodie...**(Bodie, California).

Secret Admirer

As spring awaits her arrival,
and breezes blow so subtle,
A flower begins to open.
She quietly blushes and blooms.
Her petals unfold in glorious wonder,
At a summer she once could not find.
A long, harsh winter closed her up,
But springtime changed her mind.
A soft, light breeze touches her leaves.
A faint perfume of awe seeps in.
Sudden sunlight splashes around her,
For all she can see is *him*.
This flower is but a soft-spoken girl,
Reeling in your smile.
In her mind, you are the spring,
You are her heart's desire.
Your face is the sun, your smile, the light.
Your words are the subtle breeze.
The girl is the flower, unnoticed, unknown.
And admiring–always unseen.

–Secret Admirer

Flower at Trees of Mystery. (Klamath, California).

Ring the Bell

Here in this room, with these white-washed walls,
I lie in a slumber – a slave to helpless calls.
These white bars, evenly spaced:
My prison where I have been placed.
The sweetest of hells, with colorful hues,
And flowery smells, and songs to amuse.
I'm in my playpen, let's play hide-and-seek.
I'll count to ten – a year is a week.
Then one day I'll find you in your own little cell,
And we'll laugh together, as we ring the bell.

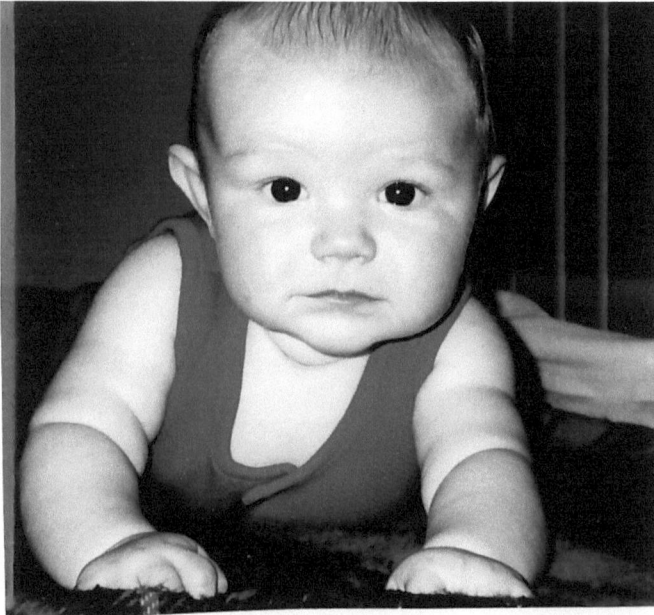

My beautiful baby & sleep robber. (Thousand Oaks, CA, 2001)

Subjugated

So I joined the masses in this orderly chaos,
Without being told the consequences.
That I would lose myself, my identity, my soul:
This, the price of their consensus.
I wanted to belong to the ranks of the righteous,
Who seemed to have the secret of life.
Instead I found death in a form, licentious:
Hypocrisy that cut me like a knife.
This blood of mine spilled, it pooled at my feet.
My heart became filled with anger and defeat.
I could not go along, or follow your example of good.
You who supposedly adore me: you'd kill me if you could.
I am not like you, and never will be: to try was my mistake.
I cannot ignore the nature of my being: a part of me, innate.
You hate me for this insurrection. Perhaps you wish you could follow?
Your parents committed infanticide, deciding which church you should know.
So you inadvertently joined the clump. Now that life is all you have to hold.
Reside now in your safe little dump: your subjugated life, empty and cold.

Interesting message…(Lebanon, Oregon).

R.I.P.

We received the education to keep ourselves afloat.
But many are not happy on this sickly '90s boat.
The '60s keep coming back, seemingly to gloat.
Many have decided to ignore these riddled days.
They simply are not willing to change their wild ways.
So it goes, their lifeblood flows. They are seemingly masochistic.
For a cheap thrill, they pop a pill, and soon become a statistic.

Sad, lone boat memorial. Morro Bay Harbor. (Morro Bay, California).

State of Being

grasping at substance, fingers crossing through air.
pulling down a step, feet meeting ground.
stepping up, the ledge is not there.
a wax fruit. Of music, not sound.
I'm lost whenever I think of him.
lost, not found, it's sink or swim.
this tragedy's careening,
to want when unwanted.
these thoughts have no meaning,
to need when unneeded.
my words lay unseeded,
to care when not cared for.
my heart is unseated,
to love when unloved.
offered up and unclaimed.
this is my state of being.
professed and maimed.
soul possessed and unseeing.

Entrance to Deepwood Estate Historical Museum. (Salem, OR).

Best Thing

Waiting around, feeling down, my head bent to the ground.
Feeling sad, a little mad, how did it all come to this?
Who knew what could come from a kiss?
Would it be that bad? Would it really be that sad?
This could be the best thing I've ever had.
What should I do? It may not even be true.
A little bit of me and you. How can this be?
It can't happen to me. I'll just have to wait and see.
Would it be that bad? Would it really be that sad?
This could be the best thing I've ever had.
Mommy, dear, would you understand my fear?
I know long ago, you were here. What would you say?
If I told you today? What would you do?
I made the same mistake as you.
And, oh, my dear, I know you want it to disappear.
Yet, you say that you love me sincere.
Would it be that bad? Would it really be that sad?
This could be the best thing I've ever had.
Still up in the air, for me and you.
I could be one, for you: or Two.
Oh, my love, what would you do?
Would it be that bad? Would it really be all that sad?
This could be the best thing I've ever had.
It could be the best thing I've ever done.
No longer being just one. I can't undo what we have done.
This could be the best thing we've ever had.
Would it really be that bad? I'll be a Mom, and you'll be a Dad.
Is it all that sad? This will be the best thing I've ever had.
And in the end, I think I'm glad.

She (and my son) really are the best things I've ever had. And I'm *far more* than glad.

The Day I Lost

I have been hit, screamed at, yelled at, and abused.
Cheated on, stolen from, deceived, and used.
Manipulated, frustrated, made to feel ashamed.
Misunderstood, ignored and commonly ill named.
I have been trapped, affection-starved, and caged.
Walked on a leash, force fed, and against-my-will
engaged. Looked down upon, placed on a pedestal, prized
and claimed. Controlled, enrolled, had my emotions
maimed. Been disregarded, disassembled, sneered at, and
appraised. I've lived a life on the edge of Hell while being
raised. But the worst pain I ever felt...
Was the day I lost you.

Hidden Beach behind Motel Trees. (Klamath, California).

Foreshadowing

There's a towering inferno about to fall. It's an unknown fate: known by all. It's born the truth, by book it's sworn. It's in the air: we've all been warned. Death and destruction, forever more. It's nothing new: we knew it before. Death and destruction, we kill and kill. The sun rises and shines, still. But there comes a day we find our fate. After the fighting, beyond the hate. To the limit, we've done our worst. Now our land, our lives are cursed. The lakes are dead, forests burned. Long since the stinking waves churned. Wretched beasts fall and die. The survivors fall to the ground and cry. Ugly sores, and burnt skin. All now unable to bear any kin. A desert land, never again green. Dark clouds, the blue sky never seen. Technology wasted, stupidity used. Earth, charity, and love: abused. It's coming, it's coming: we knew it before. Brace yourselves, humanity. Brace yourselves for the War.

Last Sunset at Ruby Beach. (Quinault, Washington).

Land of You

As soon as I wrote it, it came into being.
Touch you or not, you remain, unseeing.
This distance lends no path, no chance.
Close this space, and change your stance.
For the time it would take to topple me.
Every inch, touching, revealing.
Let you into the depth of my sea.
Last vestige of my pride, I'm appealing.
Start off gently, caressing and kissing.
Salt on my skin; stroking and licking.
Making sure comfort is missing.
Show no remorse as I begin kicking.
Strong hands won't relent; I'm a storm inside.
Find my tempest with your expert eyes.
It's all right, for I know you've lied.
Stake your claim and take your prize.
These few heated moments will hold all time.
I'll be empty again, when it's through.
Returned to silence, and solitude,
In a world where I never had you.
This is my undoing. This is how it goes.
This is how it always would be.
This is my death; I'm in the throes;
In the Land of You Don't Love Me.

A beautiful sky. (Salem, Oregon).

54

The Other Side

I'll see you on the other side, where secrets do not exist.
Where time stands still, and distance subsides. Where love is never
missed. Should my life become a Hell, bad luck would come in vain.
On an audio band, you take my hand, and lead my home again.
To a place no one else can see. Not found on any map.
A place in my heart, you've discovered an art, a faculty to tap.
You reach into my soul and touch a place you've seen before.
Do you recognize that behind my eyes awaits an open door?
Stepping through, into me/into you. The trip takes just a short while.
And when we're through, there's nothing to do, but live for days on a
smile…I never know when I'll journey again, when I'll chance to meet
you, my friend. With a last *I love you*, and nothing to hide, I'll wait for
you on the other side…

Stained glass on the front door of the Flavel House Museum. (Astoria, Oregon).

Too Long

Seduce me, seduce me, claim me and use me.
Even abuse me; just give me some more.
Finesse me, caress me, slowly undress me.
Just don't distress me, don't show me the door.
Kick me to the floor. Hold me down; make me shriek.
Tie me up, tie me down, and take me to the brink.
Use the words of another, your best mate, or your brother.
Want YOU and no other, to do this deed.
Take my hand; strike me down. Hold your gun on me, you clown.
Then gently slide it over–In. And use your greed; I want your sin.
Hey Cyrano, I'm here, you know? Am I really all that gone?
I'm sure you know, how this will go. Don't make me wait too long.

A fire discovered left unattended. Hidden Beach behind Motel Trees.
(Klamath, California).

Torn Between

What is it about the dead of night that inspires lost souls?
Takes us into our deepest thoughts, and leaves us feeling whole?
What is it about the day that rips us from our dreams?
Yet leaves us chasing at the sun, to stitch our inner seams?
I wish I were the night itself, a dark and stealing thief.
To spy on those who dare remain awake to feel their grief.
To see the faces of those like me, who think they are alone.
These boundless strangers, who strike a beat and hum a lulling
tone. They know the day as well as the night, and that is why they
see. What a horror is our plight, to choose which one to be.

Kindred Swans on the Willamette River. (Salem, Oregon).

57

Try

Float on a gentle breeze. Emit that smell of sweet charm.
Tickle my nose; make me sneeze. If need be, twist my arm.

I'll be better for it in the end.

Pull me away from the path, worn thick where others have tread.
I do not wish to spark their wrath, so I'll simply avoid them instead.

They do not recognize a true friend.

Take me away from the ways of man; words that are hollow like screams.
So many things I do not understand, so many people ignoring their dreams.

The young speak; the old condescend.

I do not wish to speak of ideas, and wait for others to judge them.
I want to be where the inspiration is, away from the deafening tandem.

You, who have loved me, will not understand.

See how I hate your commands. You wonder why I don't let you in.
You thought it helped to hold my hand, to show me how to win.

Yes, I'm sure this is for the best.

I do not wish to second-guess. I don't wish to reconsider.
Do not bewilder me with your consequence. Your advice can only hinder.

Please take your badgering and give it a rest.

You will wonder as you walk your path, why I am suddenly not there.
You will puzzle, and in the aftermath, you'll say it's because you care.

You'll wonder what I found in the woods that you told me weren't right.
Declare the value of your goods, yet any you ask shall share your plight.

It is useless for you to cry.

Walkers on the path know only paths. Explorers know the rest of the world. While you stick to your plans and maps, I will go off path to explore.

For I have learned of the need to try.

"Rules…? I do not know this word you keep repeating." Oblivious Seagull. (Morro Bay, California).

Children's Halloween Moral

Gibble-dee, Gabble-dee, Gobble-dee, Gook!
The black cat said, "You are a crook!"
To the witch, "because you took,
something that belonged to me."

"I did no such thing," said the witch to the cat.
"Just ask Mr. Bat!"
And at that, she spat!
And flew away, laughing, "Hee, hee, hee!"

Mr. Bat flapped his wings, stretched out his claws,
and said, "Cat, I do so admired your paws.
Now tell me, what is the cause,
of you wailing this sad song?"

"I am missing my collar of rhinestone and pearl.
I was being petted by a little girl,
when the witch came by and in a whirl,
the girl and the collar were gone!"

"That wicked old witch!" said the bat to the cat.
"To steal your collar, imagine that!
I wonder where she could be at?"
And with that, the bat flew away singing a song.

He flew and flew, everywhere,
gliding, swooshing, fast through the air.
Then he spied the cat's collar, in the girl's hair,
and swooped down to snatch it off her head.

The black cat was feeling down and sad,
when Mr. Bat appeared and said, "Don't be mad
at that old witch, who's not all that bad,
For she didn't do what you said."

"I searched and searched, everywhere.

I found your collar, caught in the hair,
of that little girl, gave her quite a scare!
As I retrieved your collar for you."

"Oh, thank you so, Mr. Bat.
I really, truly appreciate that!
I don't know what
I should have done, without you."

The cat cooed and purred,
and licked Mr. Bat, who assured,
"That's all very nice, what I just heard,
But you know what you must do?"

"Next time, don't go accusing, instead,
Play detective and use your head!"
And with that, the bat fled,
Leaving the cat with his collar, to stew.

*CHM was the first official poem I wrote when I was ten, after
meeting Jack Prelutsky. He came to my school and I had a copy
of "It's Halloween" signed by him!

Pumpkin Scarecrow wood statue. (Bandon, Oregon).

Always, Alexander

From head to toe, you are perfection.
Your different looks belie your intention.
Though you remain reticent, little devil.
Hair neatly combed, or sleep-disheveled.

Your smile lights up an entire day,
Even without any words you might say.
And one tiny word from you, so sweet,
Takes anger away, and delight I meet.

Your beautiful laugh, your silly dance,
You take my breath away with a glance.
I feel moved to be near you day and night.
I cannot stay mad at you, try as I might.

I'd move heaven and earth for you,
And love you regardless of vice or virtue.
What is this strange spell you weave?
What a joy in you, I did receive.

Every day is a new surprise,
Whether full of tears, or laughing cries.
Your eyes are as bright either way.
"I love you," – words I wait for you to say.

But for now, you show me in other ways.
Needing me for work and at play.
Opening your arms for me to rush in,
You're a little flirt, with so-soft skin.

You're a devious little man, with boyish charm.
My early morning, innocent alarm.
A green sweater lies upon the floor,
You dream in my bed, with grownup snores!

This verdant garment could be a doll's,

A little man's warmth, so big, yet so small…
You are my breath, my reason to be.
I will carry you in my heart for eternity.

And though in time you'll roam far and wander,
My incredible wonder, should you ever ponder?
Beautiful boy, Should you doubt as you meander,
Please know that I love you *always*, Alexander.

My amazing son (and his green sweater). Preschool at Christmas time, 2003. (Thousand Oaks, California).

I Wanna Talk Like Good Will Hunting

I wanna talk like Good Will Hunting. Come up with some lines that are truly brilliant. I mean, I never really say anything funny, or something remotely resilient.

Especially when trying to make jokes, or come up with stuff on the fly. Usually, when I talk, I feel like a dummy. I mean, 'How do you like them apples?' That shit was fuckin' funny!!

Witty pick-up lines, while leaving a bar, about eating caramels and drinking coffee, and how arbitrary they both are.

Again, that was wicked smart, and that sure as hell ain't me. I wanna corner a saying or phrase, like, "Are you talkin' to *me*?"

I wanna be quoted and forever remembered, for dialogue attributed to my intelligence. But I never know what to say. Like that wicked-ass monologue that Will delivers, about why he shouldn't work for the NSA.

A little Woody Allen or Neil Simon style, thrown into the mix, it'd be the best of all frickin' worlds. I wanna throw back and forth some quick and witty banter, like that mother and daughter on The Gilmore Girls.

I wanna walk into some place and own it, and show some bully up hard. Smack them down about paying for Harvard, instead of late fees on their public library card.

Again, that shit was brilliant; it made everyone laugh in the theater. That kid was a genius, and I'm over here, just trying to come up with a one-liner.

But I'm not smart; I'm actually kinda shy. And I have no problem coming up with a rhyme.

Sitting down at my monitor, laying out the lines, trying to stream it from my head, but the perfect thread takes time. And revision and deletion, and rehearsal and final completion.

In live conversation, with no contemplation, It's um's and ah's, silence and pause, even blushing and looking at the floor. I am NOT Good Will Hunting, or badass Travis Bickle, or Lorelei or Rory Gilmore.

So if I can't be smart, maybe I could try pretty? But I ain't twenty no more, and I sure ain't skinny. Got a deviated septum, some crooked bottom teeth, and I've pulled out a few grey hairs as well. And when I do talk, it ain't like a lady; I love to swear, in case you can't tell.

I hope there's no kids present at this venue, last thing I need is some self-righteous Mommy coming over to yell. Because I'm a Mommy as well.

Hence the sagging breasts, the leftover belly fat, and thunder thighs from Hell.

My last name is Word, in case you haven't heard, and I'm keeping it forever more. Even though the guy who gave it to me walked right out the fuckin' door.

My last name's the same as my two sweet babies, and my love for them has saved me. It's changed me, made me better. A real go-getter. And a striver.

Not quite as no-nonsense, however, as that crazy Taxi Driver.

But I am a gal who faces her fears, including getting up here, talking into a mic, about my fears and my life, my hardships and strife.

About how I ain't a pretty woman like in that movie we all know, and conversations with my daughter are not like on that show.

But I am who I am, my life is what it is, and no one can take it from me. You can laugh, or yell, or think what you will, I don't care, you can even shun me.

I love myself, I like my life, I'm happy for the most part; so go ahead and front me. But I do still wish that I could talk like Good Will Fucking Hunting.

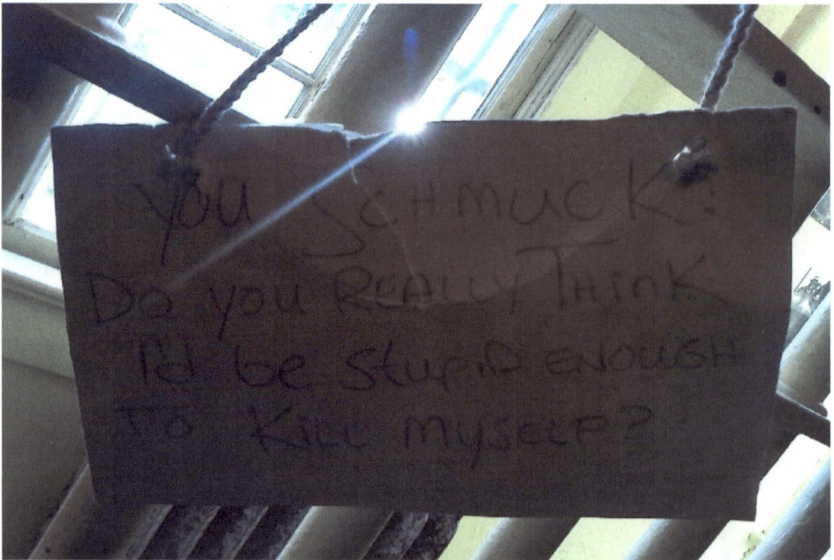

Cool stuff at *The Goonies* movie exhibit at the Oregon Film Museum. (Astoria, Oregon).

–Sparkler–

Firecrackers in pitch black skies, ideas too bright and fast to find.
Sudden light in ether and size, and despair falling close behind.
Small notions, like embers, spark, inside this maze inside my mind.
Fireflies of sand; grains too small, slip through my hand, lead me to fall.
This weight on my head bears fruit that makes me sore.
But I feel numb instead, a fire smothered in my core.
My efforts lost; I'm too weak to stand.
Totems carved with a dull knife. My fingers paint them vague and bland.
These rotted fruits stink up my life. My thoughts are not willing to resign,
But these structures of fading light are sharper than my art's design.
These rusted tools; no match for their might. The knotted wood is
cracked en masse.
Their weight remains, with messages scattered, that say: "This too shall
pass…"
But I'm still here; a leftover thought that no one has.
Not even me. I cease to be.
Blinded by my pyrotechnics.

–A sparkler gone into the sea–

Sunset at Ruby Beach. (Quinault, Washington).

Entombed

We are spirits in the flesh, **entombed**.
Bound on this plain of **life**,
To live what can only be deemed a **dream**.
Soon to slumber in an endless **dream of nothing**.
This life, this dream is all we have to *forget*.

One chance to either *fuck up* or get it right.
But if I'm gonna do it, I'm gonna **do it from the heart**,
With **no shame** or regret.
For my spirit was **born a dreamer** into this life,
And I know no other way to **see these visions**.

I only know how to dream, to want, to **strive for it all**:
Even the **impossible**.
To buck and **scream**, to **protest** silence.
To **laugh** in the face of *no*,
And *can't*, and *not good enough*.

To **shed this cloak** of *crazy*, and don a dress of
daring.
I **embrace** my **spontaneity**, my *carelessness*,
My *indecisive* and *reckless* **attitude**.
I'll *never* live with words like, **I wish I had**,
or **I always wanted to**.

Opinions may form; friends will come and go,
The world might *judge me harshly*, but—
I **laughed** 'til I cried, I **cried** 'til I fell unconscious,
I **yelled** instead of holding it in, and I loved **fiercely**,
Undeniably, and I **spat** in the face of rejection.

I *delighted* with all of my heart & I ***danced with my demons***.

I am a spirit in the flesh, ***entombed***.
Bound on this plain of ***life***,
To live what can only be deemed ***my dream***.
If others would ***grace*** it and ***dance with me***,
I should consider *them* ***lucky***.

Burial tomb at Ferndale Cemetery. (Ferndale, California).

About the Poet

Jennifer Word was born and raised in Anchorage, Alaska, and currently lives in Salem, Oregon with two cats, and occasionally her two teenagers. Aside from the ability to talk like good Will Hunting someday, her aspirations are to live a simple life and continue documenting her travels and life highlights through amateur photography and random jotted lines. That and she'd also like to read everything Stephen King has ever written before she dies. She's currently less than halfway through that one. Here's her actual writer's bio:

All Because of the Cat & Other Tales was Jennifer's debut short fiction collection, published May 16, 2015. This was quickly followed up by her debut novel, Once More, a Mature YA Paranormal Romance, on June 17, 2015.

Jennifer is an amazingly prolific author. She's currently working on several new projects, including four new novels and a debut Poetry & Photography Art anthology. We can't wait to see what imaginative yarn she weaves next.

Jennifer has a B.A. degree in Psychology from Pepperdine University, with minors in Education and English. Previously a Lovaas Therapist specializing in work with Autistic children, Jennifer now works as a

Copy Editor for Perpetual Motion Machine Publishing. She recently founded her own publishing company, EMP Publishing, and also works as an independent contract editor through her company.

Jennifer is an award winning poet. Her short stories, flash fiction and poetry have appeared in *The Storyteller, The Klondike Sun, Dark Eclipse, Surreal Grotesque, eFiction,* and multiple anthologies, including: *Slices of Flesh; Zombies Need Love, Too; Frightmares;* and *From Beyond the Grave*.

You can follow her new releases through her author website: http://www.jenniferwordauthor.com and also follow her company's latest releases at: http://www.emppublishing.com.

www.ingramcontent.com/pod-product-compliance
Lightning Source LLC
Chambersburg PA
CBHW041529090426
42738CB00035B/11